EXPLORING DINOSAURS & PREHISTORIC CREATURES

MEGALOSAURUS

By Susan H. Gray

THE CHILD'S WORLD®
CHANHASSEN, MINNESOTA

Published in the United States of America by The Child's World®
PO Box 326, Chanhassen, MN 55317-0326
800-599-READ
www.childsworld.com

Content Adviser:
Peter Makovicky,
PhD, Curator,
Field Museum,
Chicago, Illinois

Photo Credits: ML Sinibaldi/Corbis: 6; Bettmann/Corbis: 11; Jonathan Blair/Corbis: 24; Mansell/Time Life Pictures/Getty Images: 17; Nat Farbman/Time Life Pictures/Getty Images: 19; Linda Hall Library of Science, Engineering & Technology: 18; The Natural History Museum, London: 5, 7, 8, 9, 12, 20, 25; Sheila Terry/Photo Researchers, Inc.: 13, 15; Roger Harris/Science Photo Library/Photo Researchers, Inc.: 22; Chris Butler/ Photo Researchers, Inc.: 23; David R. Frazier/Photo Researchers, Inc.: 26.

The Child's World®: Mary Berendes, Publishing Director

Editorial Directions, Inc.: E. Russell Primm, Editorial Director; Katie Marsico, Associate Editor; Ruth Martin, Line Editor; Judith Shiffer, Assistant Editor; Matt Messbarger, Editorial Assistant; Susan Hindman, Copy Editor; Melissa McDaniel, Proofreader; Olivia Nellums, Fact Checkers; Tim Griffin/IndexServ, Indexer; Dawn Friedman, Photo Researcher; Linda S. Koutris, Photo Selector

Original cover art by Todd Marshall

The Design Lab: Kathleen Petelinsek, Design and Page Production

Library of Congress Cataloging-in-Publication Data
Gray, Susan Heinrichs.
  Megalosaurus / by Susan H. Gray.
    v. cm. — (Exploring dinosaurs)
  Contents: Not a good day—What is a Megalosaurus—Who discovered
Megalosaurus—The world of Megalosaurus—Telling the dinosaurs apart—Where
Megalosaurus fits in.
  ISBN 1-59296-236-X (lib. bdg. : alk. paper) 1. Megalosaurus—Juvenile literature.
[1. Megalosaurus. 2. Dinosaurs.] I. Title.
  QE862.S3G6953 2005
  567.912—dc22   2003027055

TABLE OF CONTENTS

CHAPTER ONE

NOT A GOOD DAY

Megalosaurus (MEG-uh-loe-SAWR-uhss) was out looking for breakfast. Perhaps he would find some tender young dinosaur to eat. Perhaps his meal would be an old, sickly **reptile.** Maybe he'd have to eat the remains of a dinosaur that had died last week. He lumbered along, turning his head from left to right, looking for food. At last, he spied it in the distance—a big, bulky dinosaur peacefully eating some plants. *Megalosaurus* picked up his pace.

Suddenly, he stopped in his tracks. He could not budge. He had run right into a swamp, and now his feet were stuck in the mud. *Megalosaurus* pulled and strained. He straightened his back and threw his head forward. His hands clawed the air. Still, he was stuck in place.

Megalosaurus *was a fierce prehistoric hunter. It had dangerously sharp teeth and claws and was considered to be among the more intelligent dinosaurs.*

The dinosaur twisted and squirmed about. He tried to push himself forward. He thrashed his arms. His tail slapped the mud.

Suddenly, one foot pulled loose. *Megalosaurus* took a step toward

Despite Megalosaurus's *large size, scientists believe it was probably able to move quickly. Unfortunately, speed and ferocious hunting skills were no help to the dinosaur if it got stuck in a muddy swamp such as the one shown here.*

dry land. He leaned forward again and shut his eyes tightly as every muscle strained. Finally, the other foot pulled free. *Megalosaurus* stepped forward onto damp ground. Two more steps, and he was on dry land.

His feet were covered in mud, but he was interested in something else. He looked in the direction of the plant-eating dinosaur. But the dinosaur was nowhere in sight. Breakfast had gotten away.

CHAPTER TWO

WHAT IS A MEGALOSAURUS?

Megalosaurus was a dinosaur that lived from about 185 million to 160 million years ago. Its name is taken from Greek words that mean "great lizard." Scientists know that it once lived in the area now known as England.

Like other meat-eating dinosaurs such as Tyrannosaurus rex *(tie-RAN-uh-sawr-UHSS REX) and* Allosaurus *(AL-oh-SAWR-uhss),* Megalosaurus *had a large head, short front paws, and powerful hind legs.*

Even larger plant eaters had reason to be concerned if they saw Megalosaurus *heading their way. Scientists believe* Megalosaurus's *size, speed, and razor-sharp teeth helped it to overtake bigger animals.*

Megalosaurus was an enormous creature. When fully grown, it could be as long as 30 feet (9 meters). It stood 10 feet (3 m) tall— as high as a modern-day basketball goal. An adult weighed more than a ton.

The huge reptile had two mighty legs and small but powerful arms. Each hand ended with three clawed fingers. The dinosaur had long toes with sharp claws. *Megalosaurus* walked upright on its back legs, leaning forward and holding its tail up off the ground. The dinosaur would swing its massive tail from side to side or raise and lower it to help keep its heavy body balanced.

The animal's head was huge. It had strong jaw muscles and a mouth filled with sharp teeth. The neck was thick and muscular. The bones throughout the whole body were dense and heavy. Without a doubt, this dinosaur was a powerhouse.

Megalosaurus was a meat eater, or carnivore (KAR-nih-VORE). It probably chased down slower animals, including other dinosaurs. It may also have eaten animals that had already died. Animals that do this are called scavengers (SKAV-en-jerz).

This Megalosaurus *jaw bone shows newer teeth pushing upward to replace the older ones. The dinosaur had teeth with notches similar to the grooves on a steak knife. Like a steak knife,* Megalosaurus *teeth were also capable of making deep and often deadly cuts.*

CHAPTER THREE

WHO DISCOVERED MEGALOSAURUS?

It is hard to say exactly who discovered *Megalosaurus.* That is because people found the dinosaur's bones long before they knew dinosaurs existed.

The story begins in the 1670s. A scientist named Robert Plot was writing a book about the plants and animals of Oxfordshire, England. People from all over sent him **specimens** to study or information to include in the book. Some people sent him plants and seeds. Others told him about the animals in their area. Still others gave him rocks with unusual shapes or **fossils.**

Plot was not quite sure what to make of the fossils. He had various theories about what they were. He thought some of the fossils were just beautiful shapes formed by nature.

In addition to the fame he gained finding fossils, Robert Plot also was a science professor at Oxford University in England.

One fossil, though, was clearly a piece of bone. It was part of a dinosaur's thighbone, near the knee, and it was enormous. But Plot did not know about dinosaurs. In fact, at that time no one knew about dinosaurs. He puzzled over the bone for a long time. After much thought, he decided that giant humans had once walked the earth. The mysterious bone probably came from one of them.

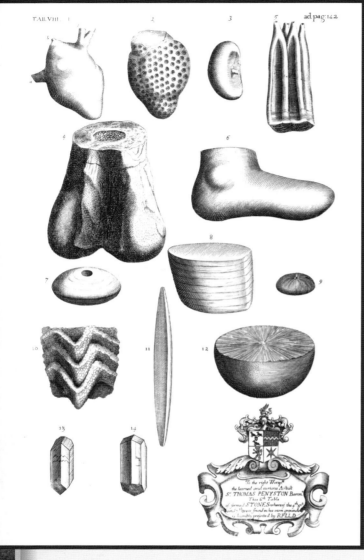

When Plot made this drawing of unusual rocks, crystals, and fossils, he included the mysterious thigh bone. Because no one at that time knew about dinosaurs, some scientists even thought the thigh bone came from an ancient elephant.

Over the next 150 years, more huge bones were discovered. Finally, another English scientist, William Buckland, took a look at them. Buckland knew they were not human bones. He decided they came from some strange reptile. He called the reptile *Megalosaurus*.

In 1842, a third Englishman, Richard Owen, became involved. He had been studying the fossils of many strange reptiles. Owen claimed that these mysterious reptiles existed

long ago but had died out. He called them dinosaurs.

So who discovered *Megalosaurus*? Was it Robert Plot, who had

its bone but thought it

was human? Was it

William Buckland, who

named it *Megalosaurus*

but didn't know it was a

dinosaur? Was it

Richard Owen, who

finally figured out that

there were dinosaurs?

You decide!

Richard Owen contributed much to our understanding of dinosaurs, and he also played an important role in the construction of Crystal Palace Park in England. This park was the first to feature life-sized models of dinosaurs.

William Buckland was one of the most unusual scientists ever. He was born in England in 1784. As a boy, he often collected fossils with his father, and he liked to study science in school. When he went to college, he continued to study science and especially liked geology.

Later, Buckland got a teaching job and gave talks about plants, animals, and the earth's history. His talks were always entertaining and were often quite dramatic. As he spoke, he paced back and forth in front of his class. Then he would leap in front of his students, thrust his face into theirs, and shout questions at them.

At home, Buckland was just as eccentric. He collected hundreds of fossils and kept them around the house. A friend came to visit him once and was shocked at the mess he saw. The friend wrote that one room ". . . was filled with rocks, shells, and bones in . . . confusion, and . . . at the end was my friend in his black gown . . . cleaning out a fossil. . . ."

Friends who were invited to dinner were often horrified to learn what was on the menu.

Word was that Buckland ate all sorts of animals. One dinner guest said that Buckland actually served toasted mice!

Although he was an unusual man, his wife and children thought he was wonderful. His wife helped him glue broken fossils together. She helped him write his scientific papers, and she drew the pictures to go with them. Buckland taught his children all about science, and he introduced them to famous scientists who came to visit.

Because Buckland was so strange, some people paid no attention to his work. They thought that he was too weird to produce anything worthwhile. They were wrong. It has been almost 200 years since William Buckland studied *Megalosaurus*. He is still known today as the very first person to name a dinosaur.

CHAPTER FOUR

THE WORLD OF MEGALOSAURUS

Megalosaurus lived during a time we call the Jurassic (jer-RASS-ik) period. At that time, the earth's great land-masses were much closer to each other than they are today. Canada and Greenland were very close to England. Africa was right next to Spain. Australia was up against the southern part of Africa. Over millions of years, these landmasses slowly drifted apart. In fact, they are still drifting today.

We know that *Megalosaurus* lived in England because its bones have been found there. However, it could be that the dinosaur also lived in Canada. Perhaps it wandered all over North America.

When the landmasses were close together, dinosaurs might have crossed from one **continent** to the next quite easily. Maybe

During the Jurassic period, which lasted 64 million years, several new dinosaur groups appeared. Even after this period ended, dinosaurs continued to walk the earth for another 79 million years.

Megalosaurus traveled from England to Canada, or from Spain to

Africa. If that is the case, we might one day find its bones in these

other places.

SOME OLD IDEAS

Back in the 1600s, scientists had a very different understanding of the world. For one thing, they were not sure what to think of fossils. Although many fossils looked like parts of animals, scientists believed this was by chance. They said that fos- sils were just examples of nature's beauty. After all, beautiful things such as crystals and snowflakes appeared in nature.

Some people knew that fossils were the remains of dead animals. However, they did not realize that some animals had become

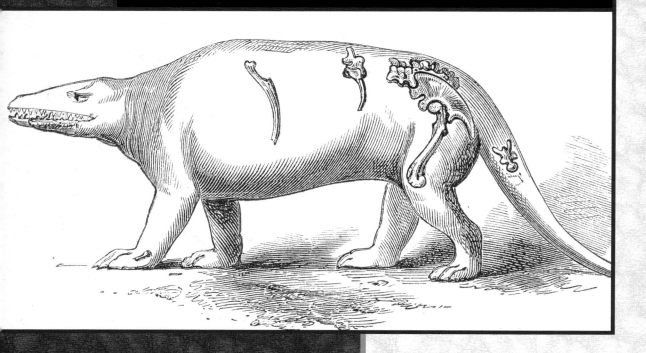

extinct. They had no idea that certain animals had simply died out. In fact, the very thought was ridiculous. These people believed that if they looked hard enough, they would find every kind of animal still living some-where on earth.

When scientists started finding dinosaur skele-tons, people really had to change their thinking. They saw that fossils were not just lovely gifts of nature. They realized that some animals had become extinct. It took years for these ideas to sink in. But at last they did, and today we know more about ancient life than we ever did before.

CHAPTER FIVE

TELLING THE DINOSAURS APART

Megalosaurus sure looked a lot like *Tyrannosaurus rex.*

And *T. rex* sure looked a lot like *Allosaurus.* They all

walked on two legs. They all had sharp teeth for eating meat.

Allosaurus (right) was one of the largest meat-eating dinosaurs in North America during the Jurassic period.

And they all had little arms. How can anyone tell them apart?

This is a problem that **paleontologists** often face. Once they know what to look for, it is not so hard. Scientists who study dinosaurs also study the rocks in which dinosaur fossils are found. They figure out the age of the rocks. The age of the rocks can give clues about the identity of the dinosaur. *T. rex* skeletons show up in rocks that are about 65 million to 67 million years old. *Megalosaurus* and *Allosaurus* are found in rocks that are more than twice that old.

Paleontologists might also look at the dinosaur's arms. *T. rex* had tiny arms. The dinosaur probably could not reach up and scratch its nose or lean over to pick up something on the ground. The other two dinosaurs also had little arms, but they were probably big enough to hold **prey** or pick at a dead animal. Also, *T. rex* had only two fingers at the end of its arms. The other two dinosaurs

Like Megalosaurus, T. rex *was a fearsome predator. This dinosaur had teeth that could grow up to 9 inches (23 centimeters) long!*

were three-fingered. If paleontologists find a dinosaur with three fingers, they know it can't be a *T. rex*.

Scientists might also look at the dinosaur's head. *Allosaurus* had a face covered with bumps, horns, and ridges. *Megalosaurus* and

T. rex were not exactly smooth-skinned, but they were not as highly

decorated as *Allosaurus.*

Paleontologists can also look at the size of the skeleton. An adult

Megalosaurus was about 10 feet (3 m) shorter than the other two.

If scientists find a skeleton that is 40 feet (12 m) long (such as the

No one is certain about the purpose of the bumps and ridges on Allosaurus's *head, but some scientists believe they may have been used to attract mates.*

Whether digging for dinosaur bones or studying them, paleontologists need to be extremely careful. Many of these fossils are delicate and can be easily destroyed if handled too roughly.

skeleton of an adult *T. rex*), they know it can't be a *Megalosaurus*—it's much too long.

When paleontologists find dinosaur bones, they compare them to bones they already know about. They study the age of the rocks around the bones. Then they try to decide which dinosaur the bones came from. Sometimes this job is easy, but sometimes it takes lots of detective work!

CHAPTER SIX

WHERE *MEGALOSAURUS* FITS IN

Today, there are millions of different kinds of animals.

Millions more lived in the past and have died out. Scientists

who study animals have a way of keeping track of all these different

kinds. They do this by sorting them into groups.

You probably know about some of the big groups already. For

Like all other creatures, prehistoric reptiles could be divided into groups. Some flew through the air and resembled birds; others swam through the water using fins and flippers. Several were plant eaters, but many hunted and ate other animals. These differences are important because they help paleontologists to identify fossil remains and also to examine relationships between prehistoric creatures and modern-day animals.

instance, all the sea jellies in the world fit in to one big group. All the different kinds of spiders fit in to another group. Reptiles have their own group, as well.

Many reptiles are now extinct. But many others, such as turtles and lizards, are still around today. All reptiles use lungs to breathe the air. Their bodies are covered with scales or plates. Almost all of them have four legs, and most lay eggs.

Megalosaurus clearly fits in with the reptiles.

Scientists break the big groups down into smaller and smaller groups. Among the reptiles, some of those smaller

Though much smaller and a little less frightening, this alligator is a relative of Megalosaurus. *Both creatures are reptiles.*

groups include the alligator group, the snake group, and the dinosaur group. *Megalosaurus* and many other extinct reptiles fit into the dinosaur group.

Within the dinosaur group, there is a smaller group called the theropods (THEHR-uh-podz). Within that group are very large theropods called carnosaurs (KAR-ne-sawrs). Carnosaurs were the dinosaurs that walked on two legs, had small arms, and ate meat. Other carnosaurs include *T. rex, Allosaurus,* and *Velociraptor* (vuh-LOSS-ih-RAP-ter).

So far, scientists have discovered thousands of different kinds of reptiles. Hundreds of these fit in to the dinosaur group. Paleontologists believe that there are hundreds more that have not even been discovered yet. Perhaps you will be the one to discover some of these unknown dinosaurs.

Glossary

ancient (AYN-shunt) Something that is ancient is very old. Paleontologists study ancient life.

continent (KON-tuh-nuhnt) A continent is one of the earth's large landmasses. *Megalosaurus* fossils have been found on the continent of Europe.

eccentric (ek-SEN-trik) Eccentric describes someone who is odd or strange, but in a harmless or charming way. William Buckland was an eccentric scientist.

extinct (ek-STINGKT) A type of plant or animal that has died out is extinct; it no longer exists. Some types of reptiles are extinct.

fossils (FOSS-uhlz) Fossils are things that are left behind by ancient plants or animals. *Megalosaurus* fossils have been found in England.

geology (jee-OL-uh-jee) Geology is the study of the earth. Geologists can tell us what our planet was like when dinosaurs lived.

paleontologists (PAY-lee-uhn-TOL-uh-jists) Paleontologists are people who study ancient living things. Paleontologists can tell us about the differences between *Megalosaurus* and other theropods.

prey (pray) Prey are animals that are hunted and eaten by other animals. *Megalosaurus* probably used its sharp claws to tear into prey.

reptile (REP-tile) A reptile is an animal that breathes air, has a backbone, and is usually covered with scales or plates. *Megalosaurus* was a reptile that is now extinct.

specimens (SPESS-uh-muhnz) Specimens are things used to represent an entire group. Robert Plot thought his *Megalosaurus* specimen was a human bone.

Did You Know?

▸ Robert Plot's original *Megalosaurus* bone has been lost. All that remains of it is a drawing.

▸ In the 1850s, a famous artist made a concrete model of *Megalosaurus* so the public could see what the creature looked like. Unfortunately, the statue showed it as a barrel-shaped dinosaur that walked on four feet.

▸ *Megalosaurus* footprints have been found in southern England.

How to Learn More

AT THE LIBRARY

Barrett, Paul. *National Geographic Dinosaurs*. Washington D.C.: National Geographic Society, 2001.

Lambert, David, Darren Naish, and Liz Wyse. *Dinosaur Encyclopedia*. New York: DK Publishing, 2001.

Palmer, Douglas, and Barry Cox (editors). *The Simon & Schuster Encyclopedia of Dinosaurs & Prehistoric Creatures: A Visual Who's Who of Prehistoric Life*. New York: Simon & Schuster, 1999.

ON THE WEB

Visit our home page for lots of links about *Megalosaurus*:

http://www.childsworld.com/links.html

NOTE TO PARENTS, TEACHERS, AND LIBRARIANS: We routinely verify our Web links to make sure they're safe, active sites—so encourage your readers to check them out!

PLACES TO VISIT OR CONTACT

AMERICAN MUSEUM OF NATURAL HISTORY
To view numerous dinosaur fossils, as well
as the fossils of several ancient mammals
Central Park West at 79th Street
New York, NY 10024-5192
212/769-5100

CARNEGIE MUSEUM OF NATURAL HISTORY
To view a variety of dinosaur skeletons, as well
as fossils related to other extinct animals
4400 Forbes Avenue
Pittsburgh, PA 15213
412/622-3131

DINOSAUR NATIONAL MONUMENT
To view a huge deposit of dinosaur bones
in a natural setting
Dinosaur, CO 81610-9724
        or
DINOSAUR NATIONAL MONUMENT (QUARRY)
11625 East 1500 South
Jensen, UT 84035
435/781-7700

MUSEUM OF THE ROCKIES
To see real dinosaur fossils, as well as robotic replicas
Montana State University
600 West Kagy Boulevard
Bozeman, MT 59717-2730
406/994-2251 or 406/994-DINO (3466)

NATIONAL MUSEUM OF NATURAL HISTORY
(SMITHSONIAN INSTITUTION)
To see several dinosaur exhibits and special
behind-the-scenes tours
10th Street and Constitution Avenue NW
Washington, DC 20560-0166
202/357-2700

The Geologic Time Scale

CAMBRIAN PERIOD

Date: 540 million to 505 million years ago
Most major animal groups appeared by the end of this period. Trilobites were common and algae became more diversified.

ORDOVICIAN PERIOD

Date: 505 million to 440 million years ago
Marine life became more diversified. Crinoids and blastoids appeared, as did corals and primitive fish. The first land plants appeared. The climate changed greatly during this peri-od—it began as warm and moist, but temper-atures ultimately dropped. Huge glaciers formed, causing sea levels to fall.

SILURIAN PERIOD

Date: 440 million to 410 million years ago
Glaciers melted, sea levels rose, and the earth's climate became more stable. Fish with jaws first appeared, as did the first freshwater fish. Plants with vascular systems developed. This means they had parts that helped them to conduct food and water.

DEVONIAN PERIOD

Date: 410 million to 360 million years ago
Fish became more diverse, as did land plants. The first trees and forests appeared at this time, and the earliest seed-bearing plants began to grow. The first land-living vertebrates and insects appeared. Fossils also reveal evidence of the first ammonites and amphibians. The climate was warm and mild.

CARBONIFEROUS PERIOD

Date: 360 million to 286 million years ago
The climate was warm and humid, but cooled toward the end of the period. Coal swamps dotted the landscape, as did a multi-tude of ferns. The earliest reptiles walked the earth. Pelycosaurs such as *Edaphosaurus* evolved toward the end of the Carboniferous period.

PERMIAN PERIOD

Date: 286 million to 248 million years ago
Algae, sponges and corals were common on the ocean floor. Amphibians and reptiles were also prevalent at this time, as were seed-bearing plants and conifers. However, this period ended with the largest mass extinction on earth. This may have been caused by volcanic activity or the formation of glaciers and the lowering of sea levels.

TRIASSIC PERIOD

Date: 248 million to 208 million years ago
The climate during this period was warm and dry. The first true mammals appeared, as did frogs, salamanders, and lizards. Evergreen trees made up much of the plant life. The first dinosaurs, including *Coelophysis*, walked the earth. In the skies, pterosaurs became the earliest winged reptiles to take flight. In the seas, ichthyosaurs and plesiosaurs made their appearance.

JURASSIC PERIOD

Date: 208 million to 144 million years ago

The climate of the Jurassic period was warm and moist. The first birds appeared at this time, and plant life was more diverse and widespread. Although dinosaurs didn't even exist in the beginning of the Triassic period, they ruled the earth by Jurassic times. *Allosaurus, Apatosaurus, Archaeopteryx, Brachiosaurus, Compsognathus, Diplodocus, Ichthyosaurus, Plesiosaurus,* and *Stegosaurus* were just a few of the prehistoric creatures that lived during this period.

CRETACEOUS PERIOD

Date: 144 million to 65 million years ago

The climate of the Cretaceous period was fairly mild. Many modern plants developed, including those with flowers. With flowering plants came a greater diversity of insect life. Birds further developed into two types: flying and flightless. Prehistoric creatures such as *Ankylosaurus, Edmontosaurus, Iguanodon, Maiasaura, Oviraptor, Psittacosaurus, Spinosaurus, Triceratops, Troodon, Tyrannosaurus rex,* and *Velociraptor* all existed during this period. At the end of the Cretaceous period came a great mass extinction that wiped out the dinosaurs, along with many other groups of animals.

TERTIARY PERIOD

Date: 65 million to 1.8 million years ago

Mammals were extremely diversified at this time, and modern-day creatures such as horses, dogs, cats, bears, and whales developed.

QUATERNARY PERIOD

Date: 1.8 million years ago to today

Temperatures continued to drop during this period. Several periods of glacial development led to what is known today as the Ice Age. Prehistoric creatures such as glyptodonts, mammoths, mastodons, *Megatherium,* and sabre-toothed cats roamed the earth. A mass extinction of these animals occurred approximately 10,000 years ago. The first human beings evolved during the Quaternary period.

Index

About the Author

Susan H. Gray has bachelor's and master's degrees in zoology and has taught college-level courses in biology. She first fell in love with fossil hunting while studying paleontology in college. In her 25 years as an author, she has written many articles for scientists and researchers, and many science books for children. Susan enjoys gardening, traveling, and playing the piano. She and her husband, Michael, live in Cabot, Arkansas.